TIKI GARDENS

A Coloring Book For Adults, Cool Kids or the Tragically Hip

PUBLISHED BY
CLUB TIKI PRESS
AN SLG PUBLISHING COMPANY

TIKI ILLUSTRATIONS BY
JEF BAMBAS

EDITED BY
JEF BAMBAS AND DAN VADO

SLG Publishing/Club Tiki Press
44 Race Street San Jose, CA 95126

www.clubtiki.com
www.slgcomic.com

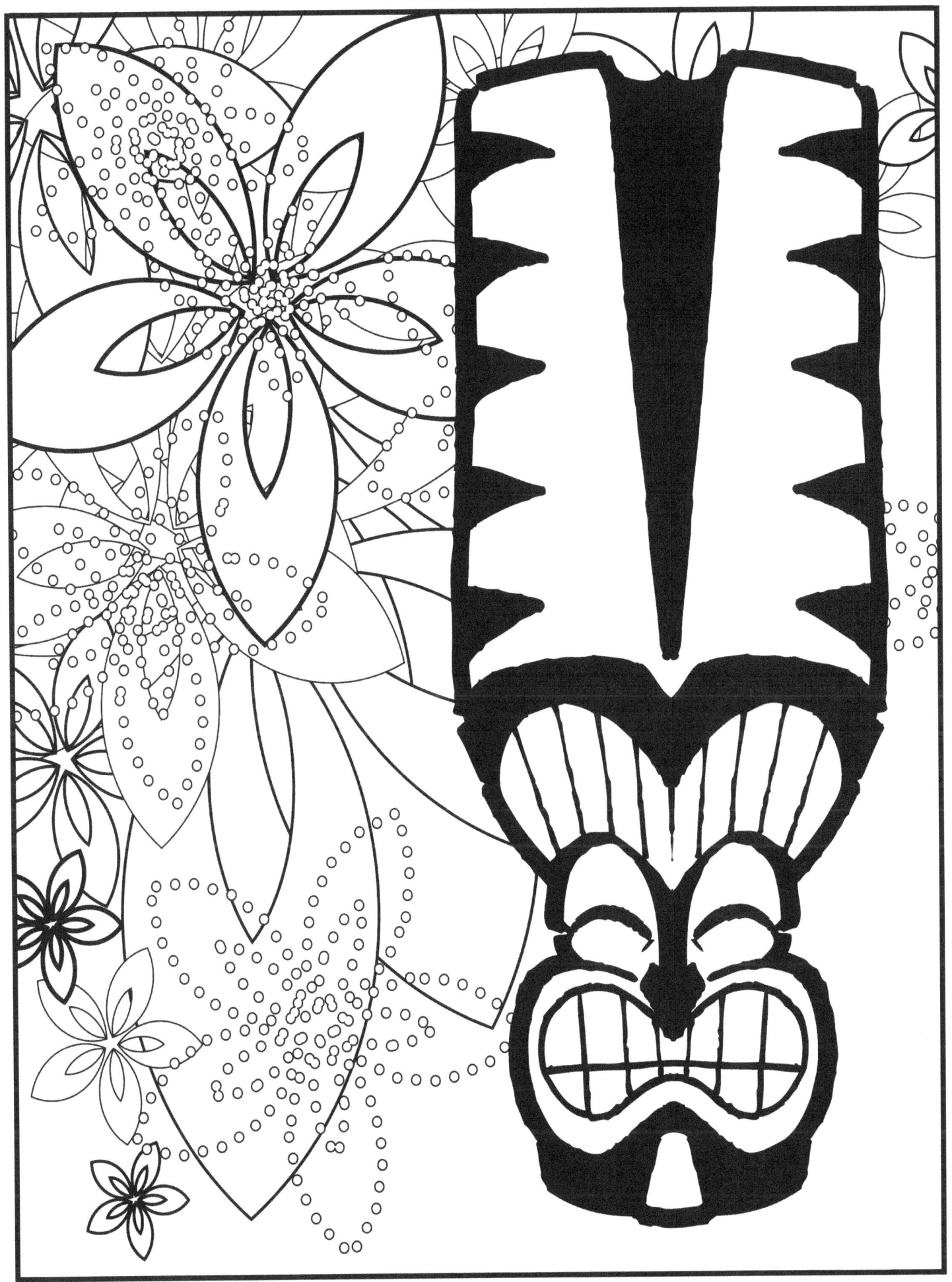

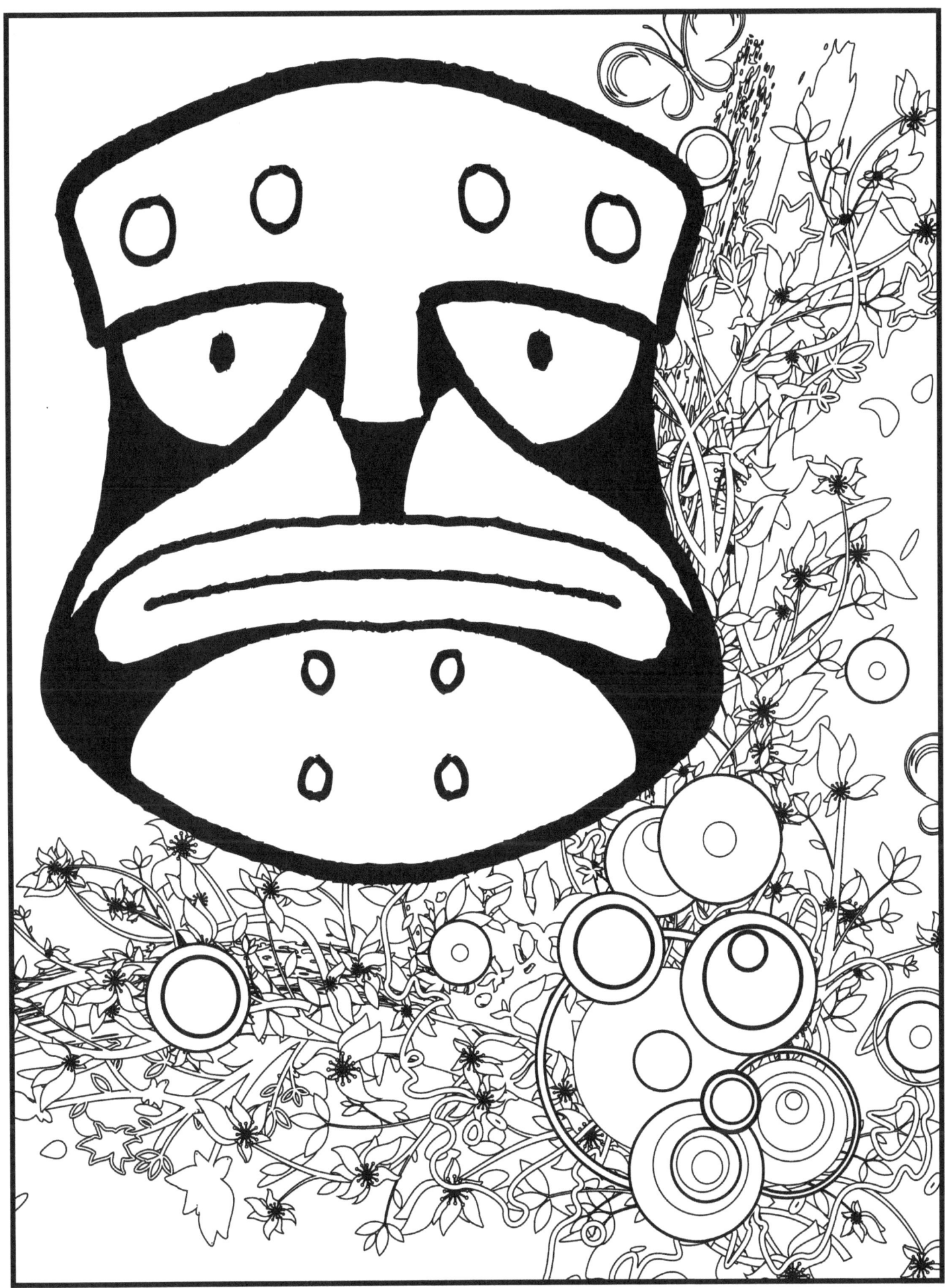

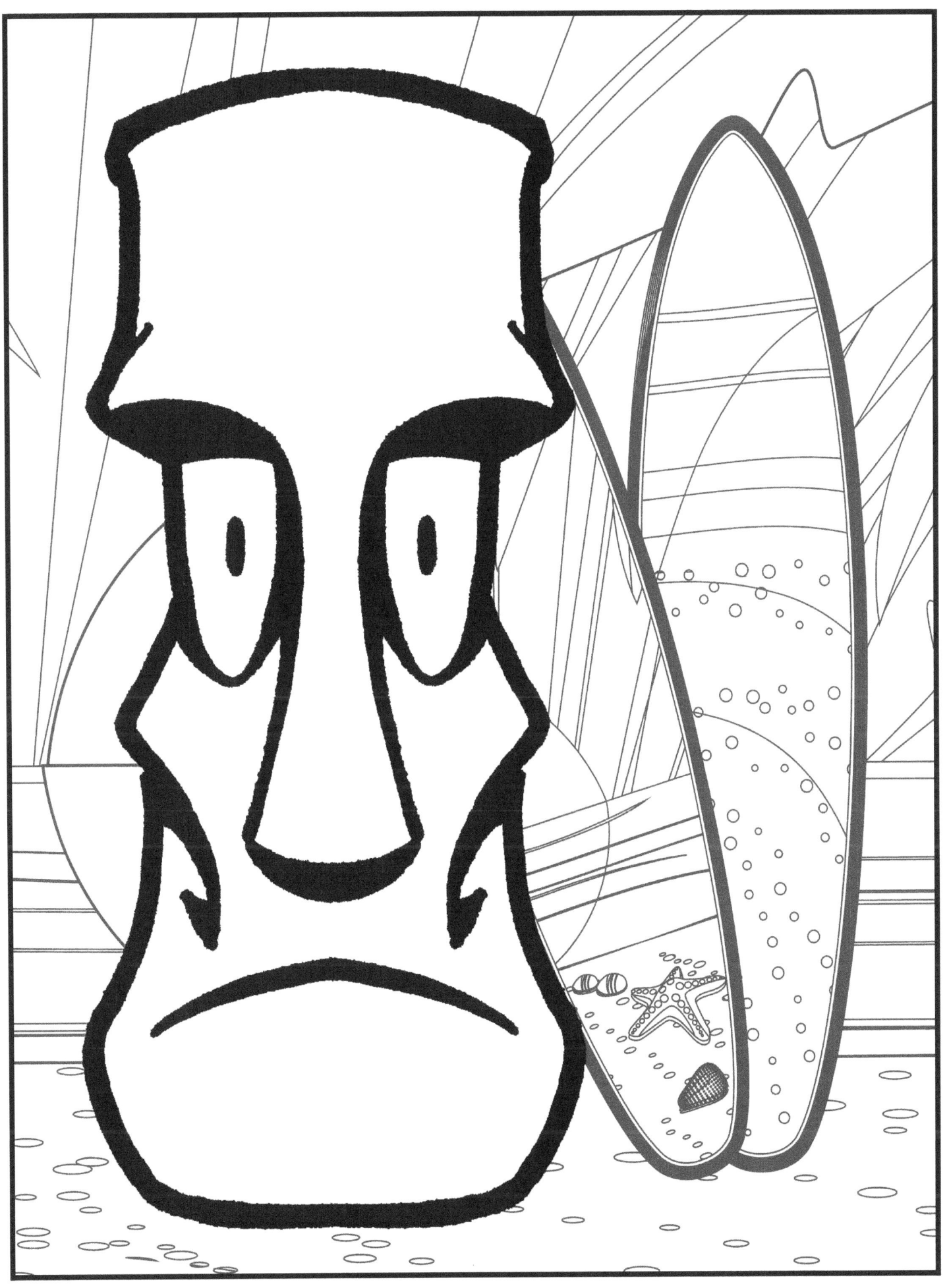

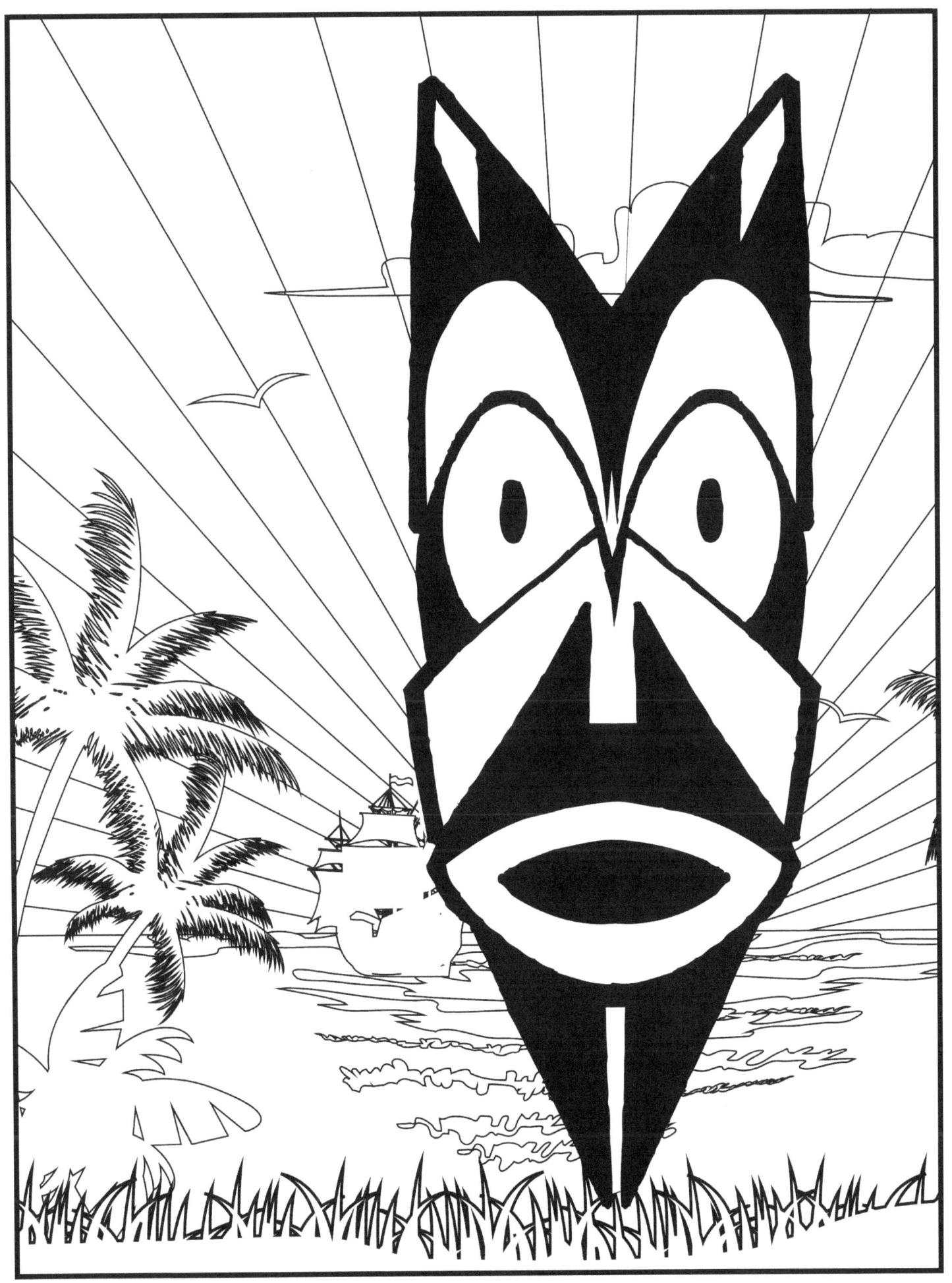

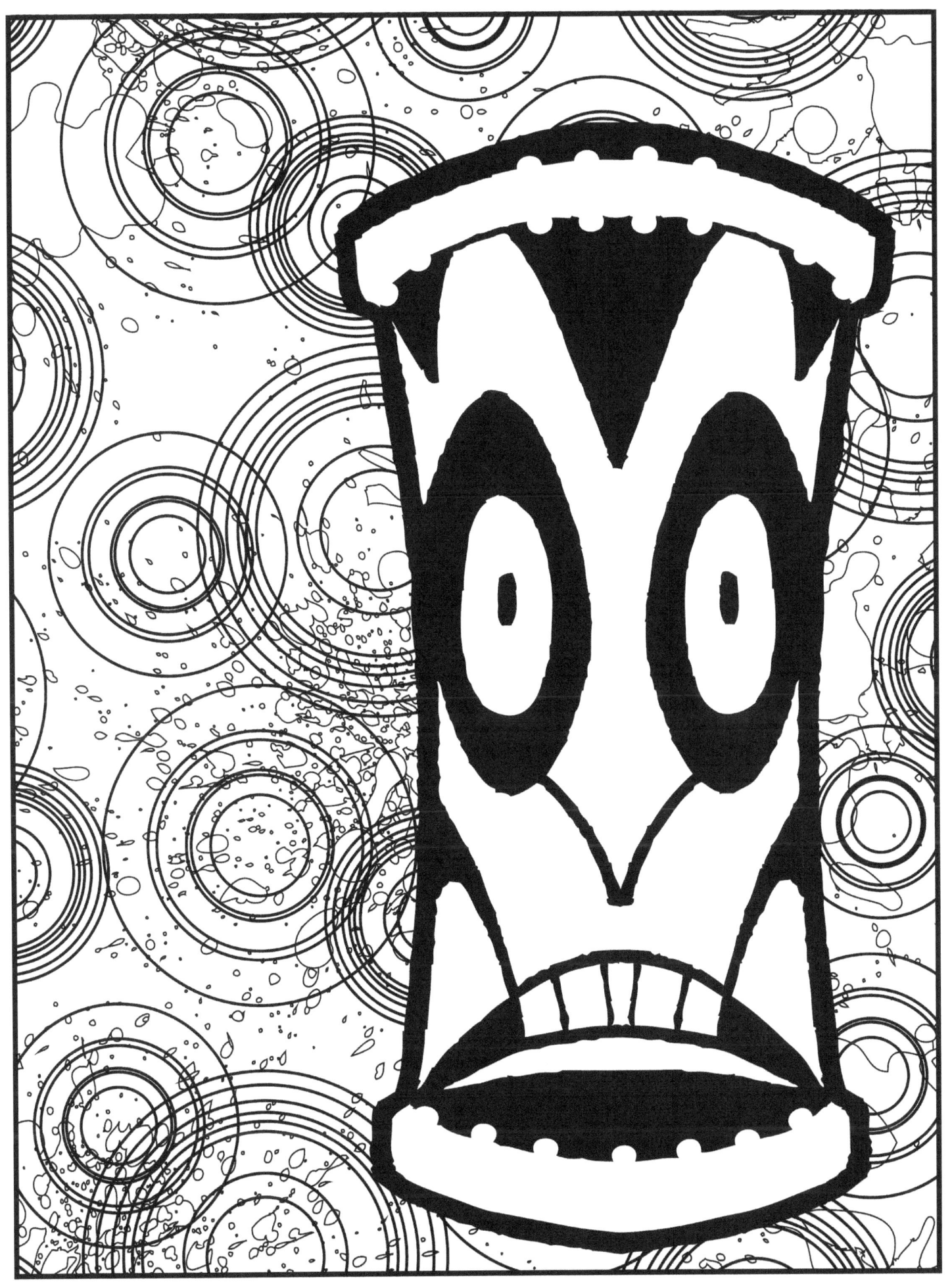

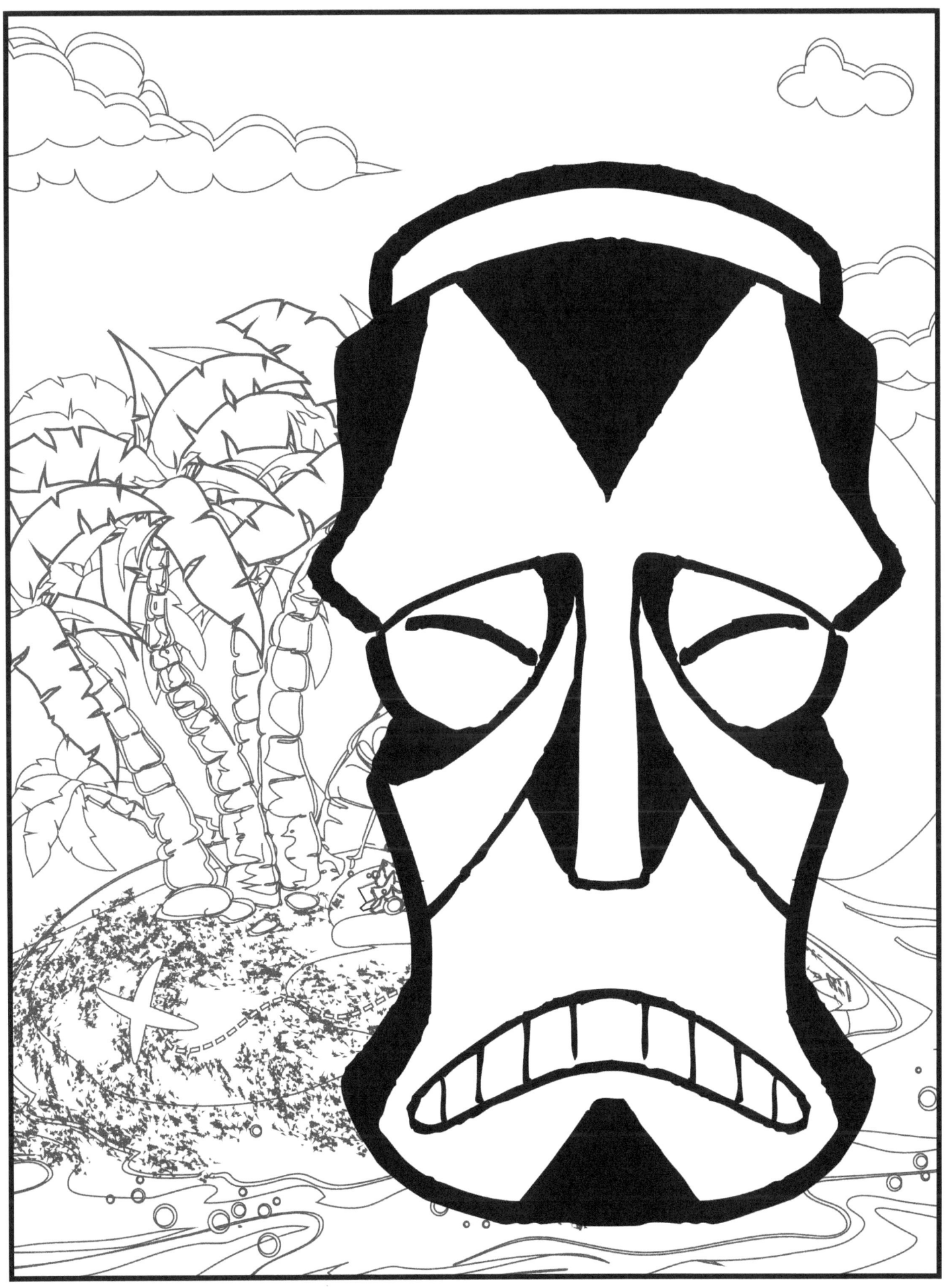

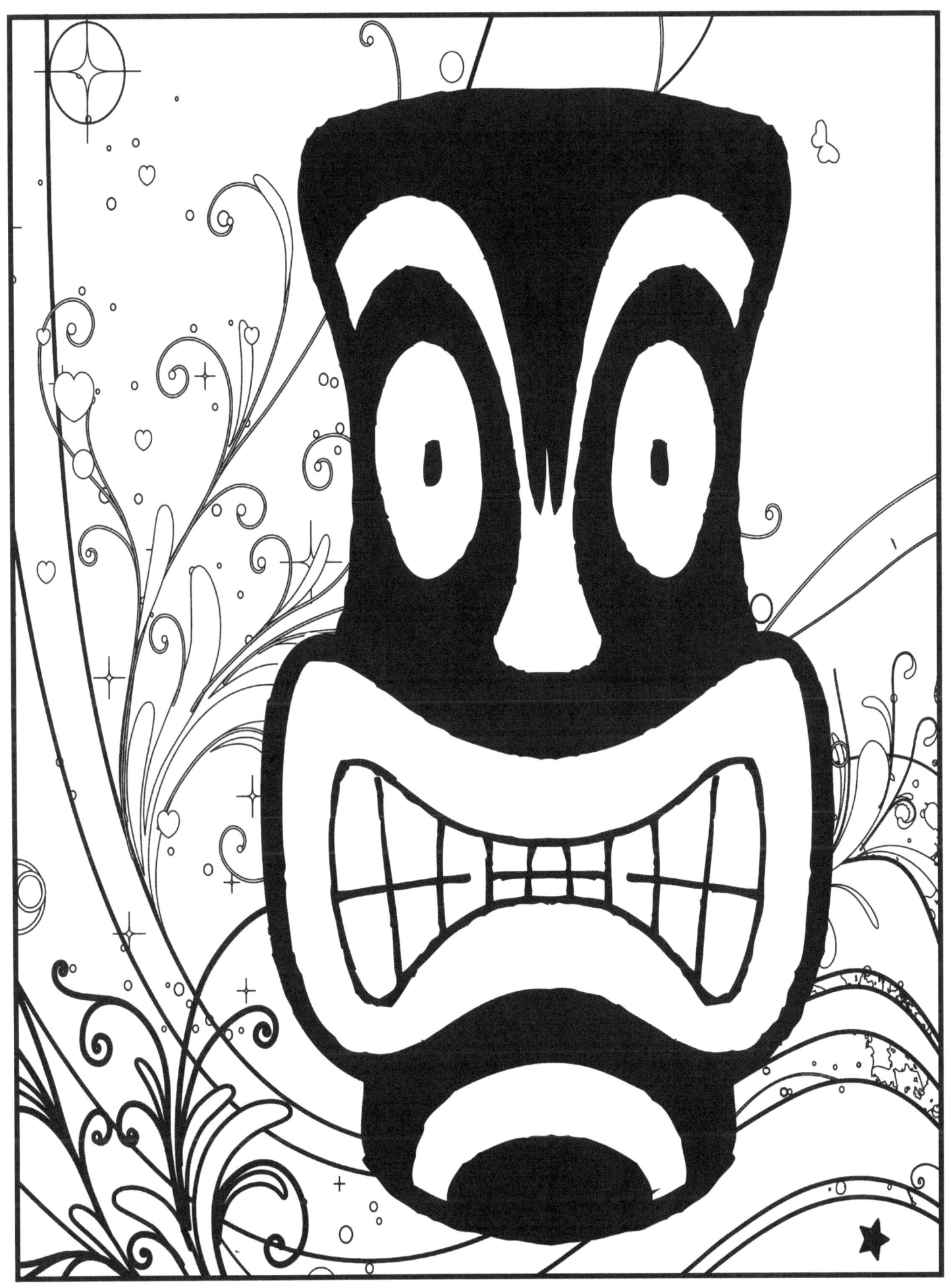

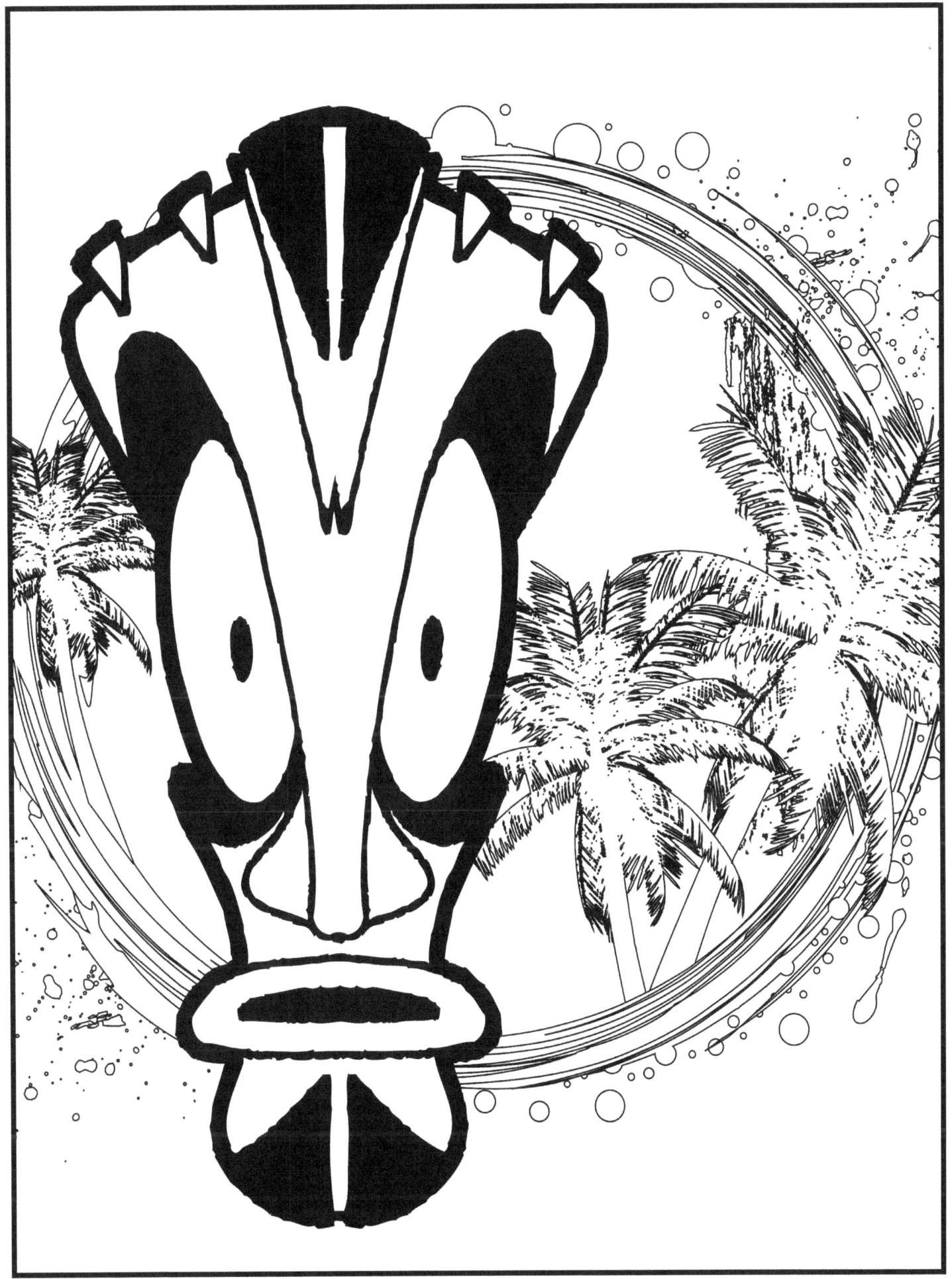

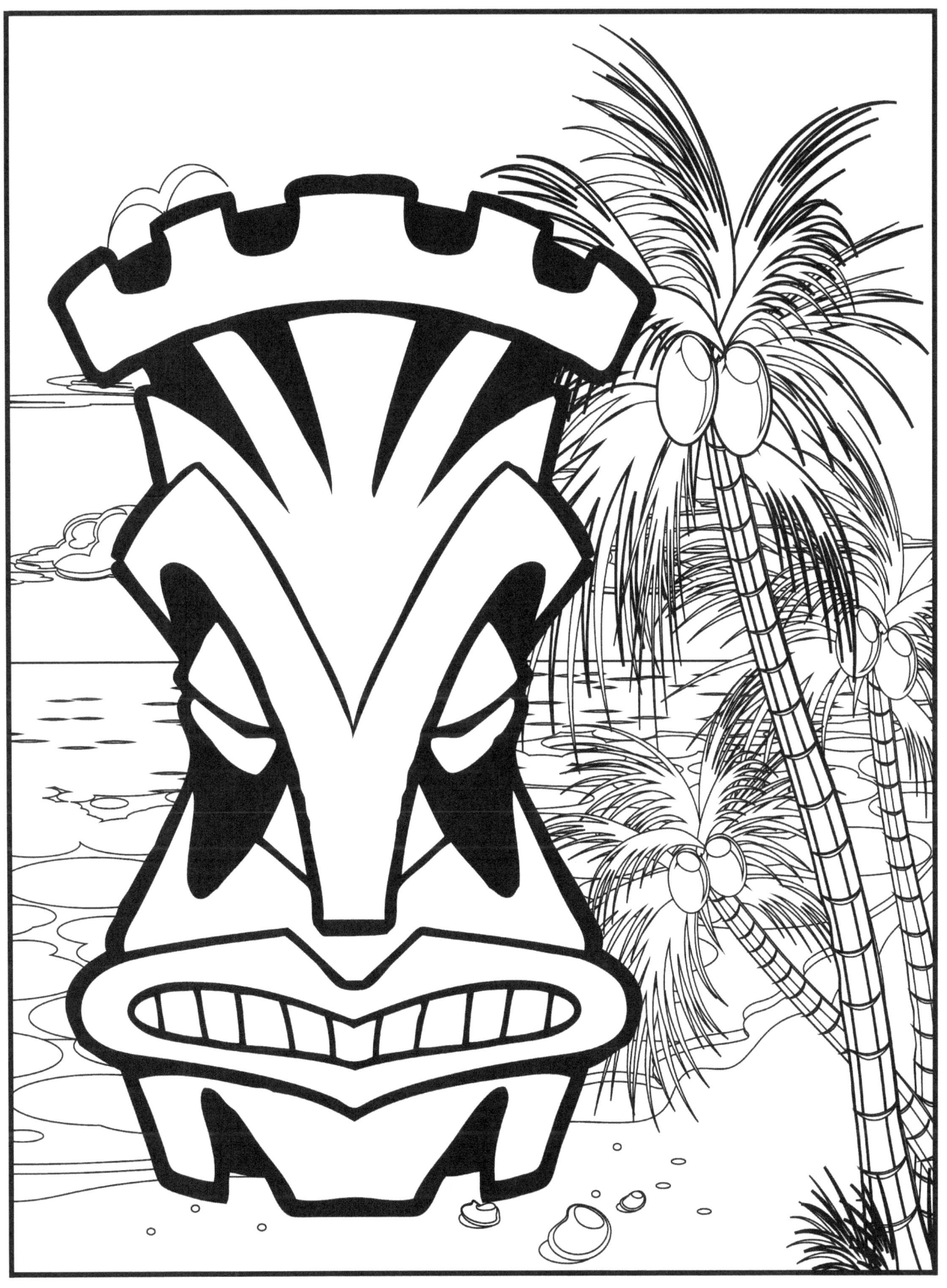

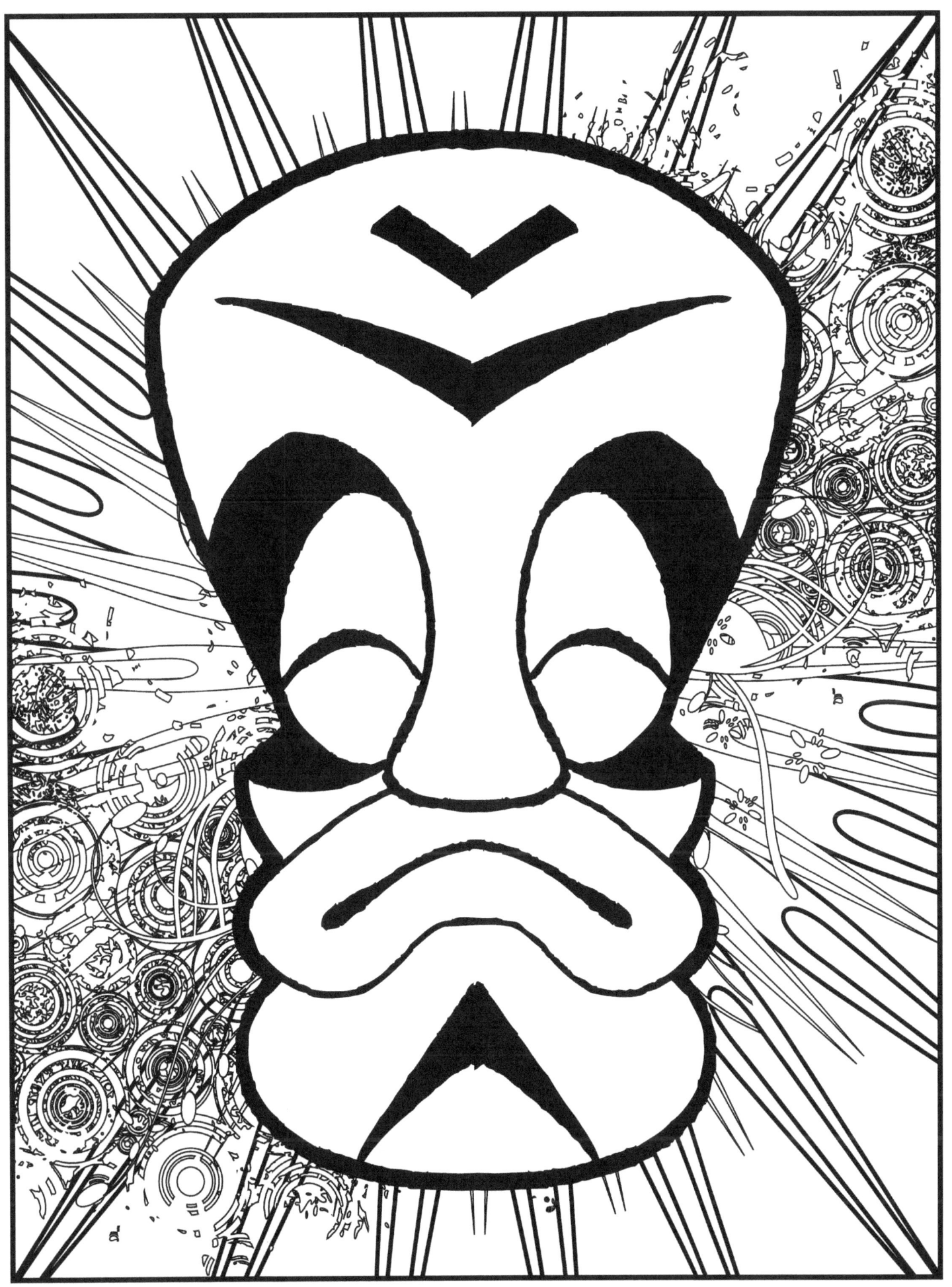

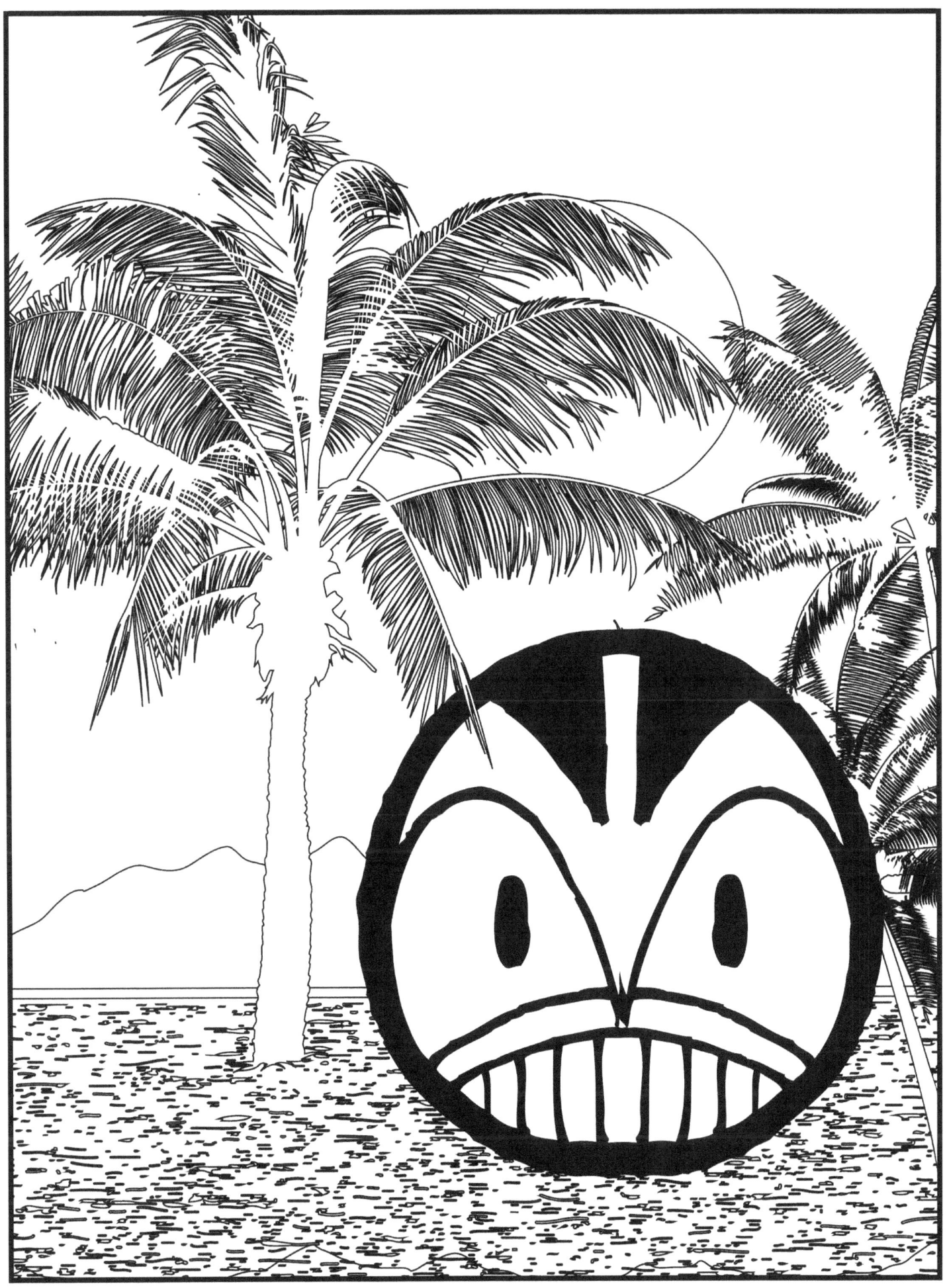

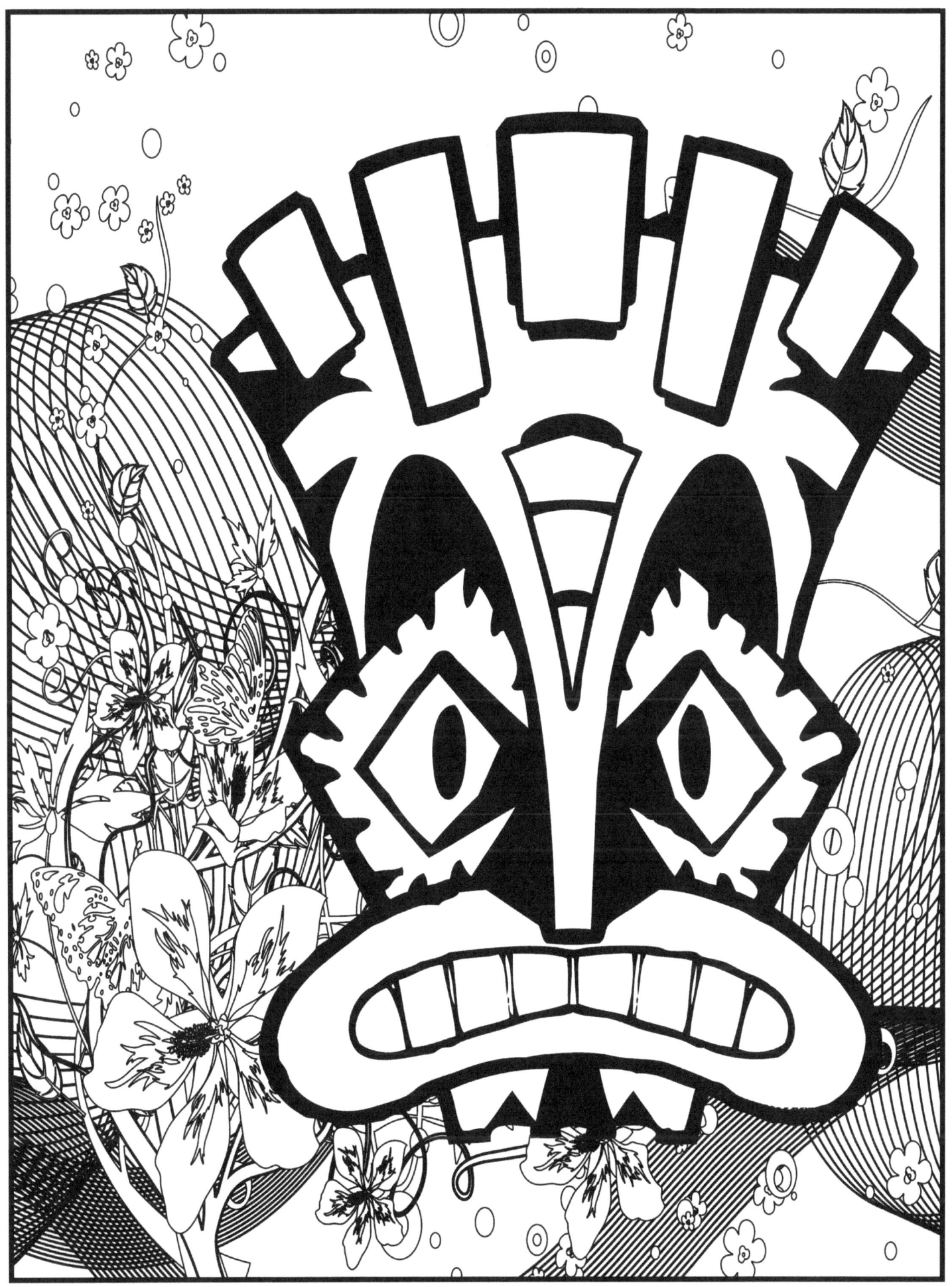

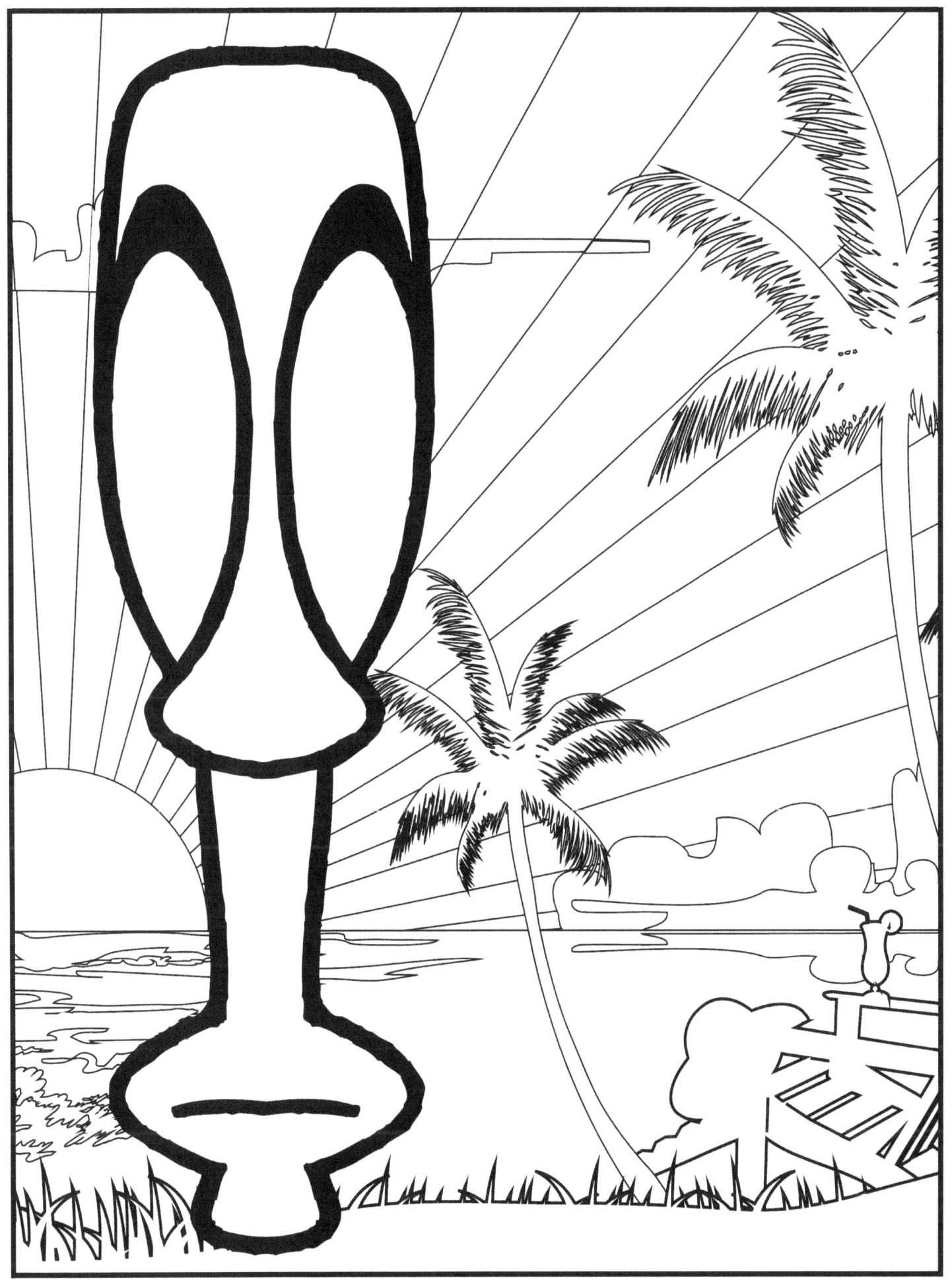

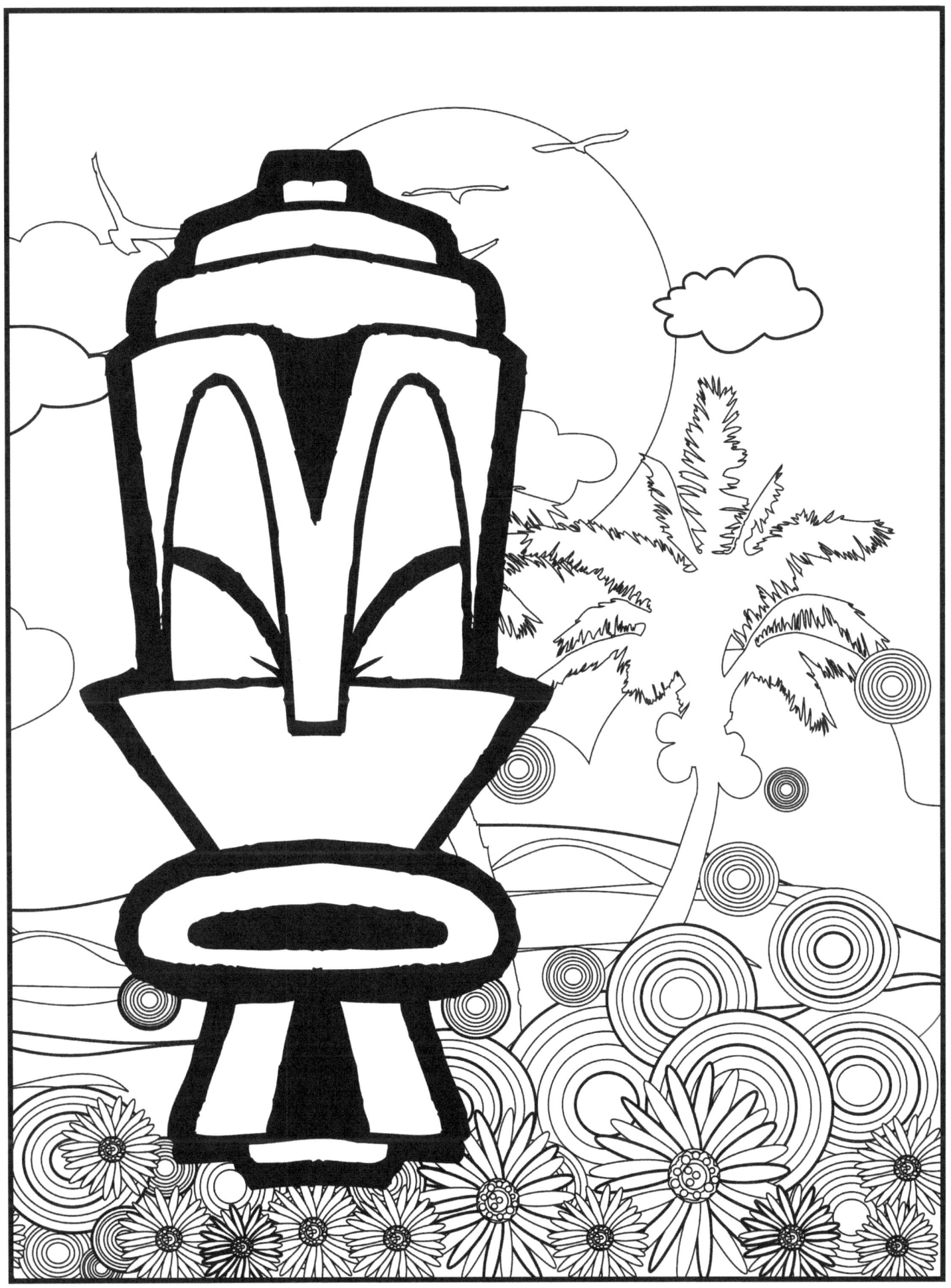

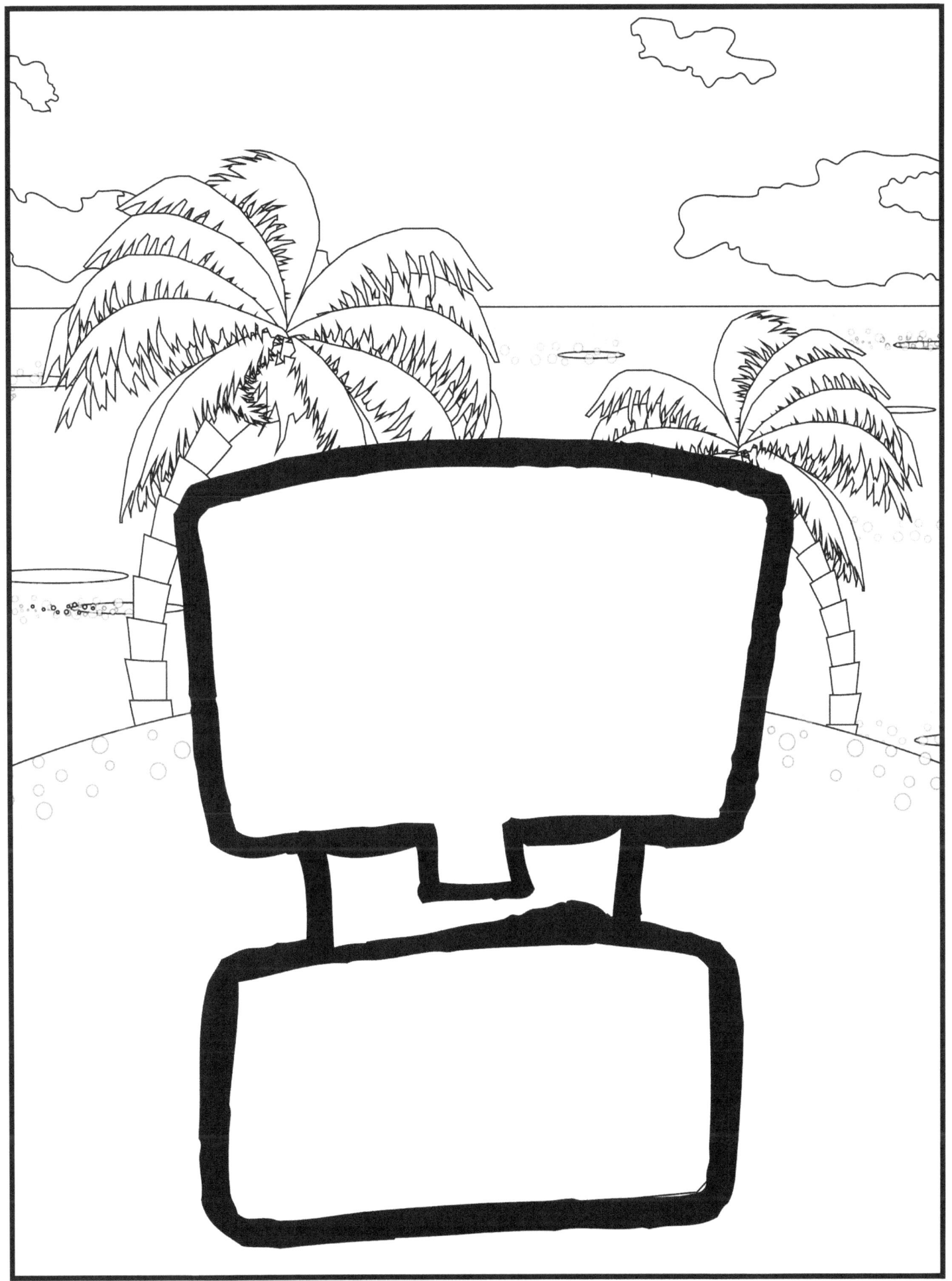

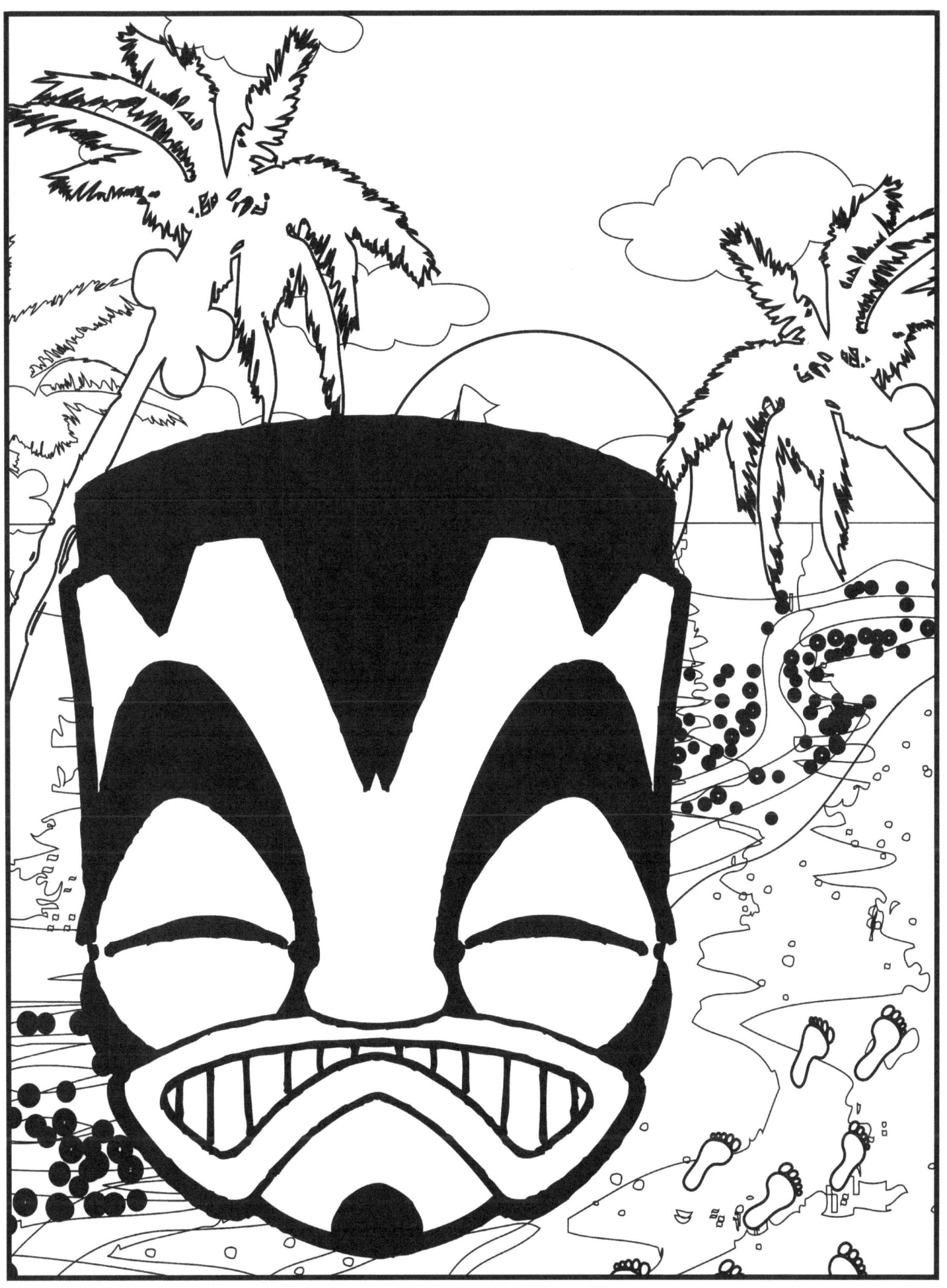

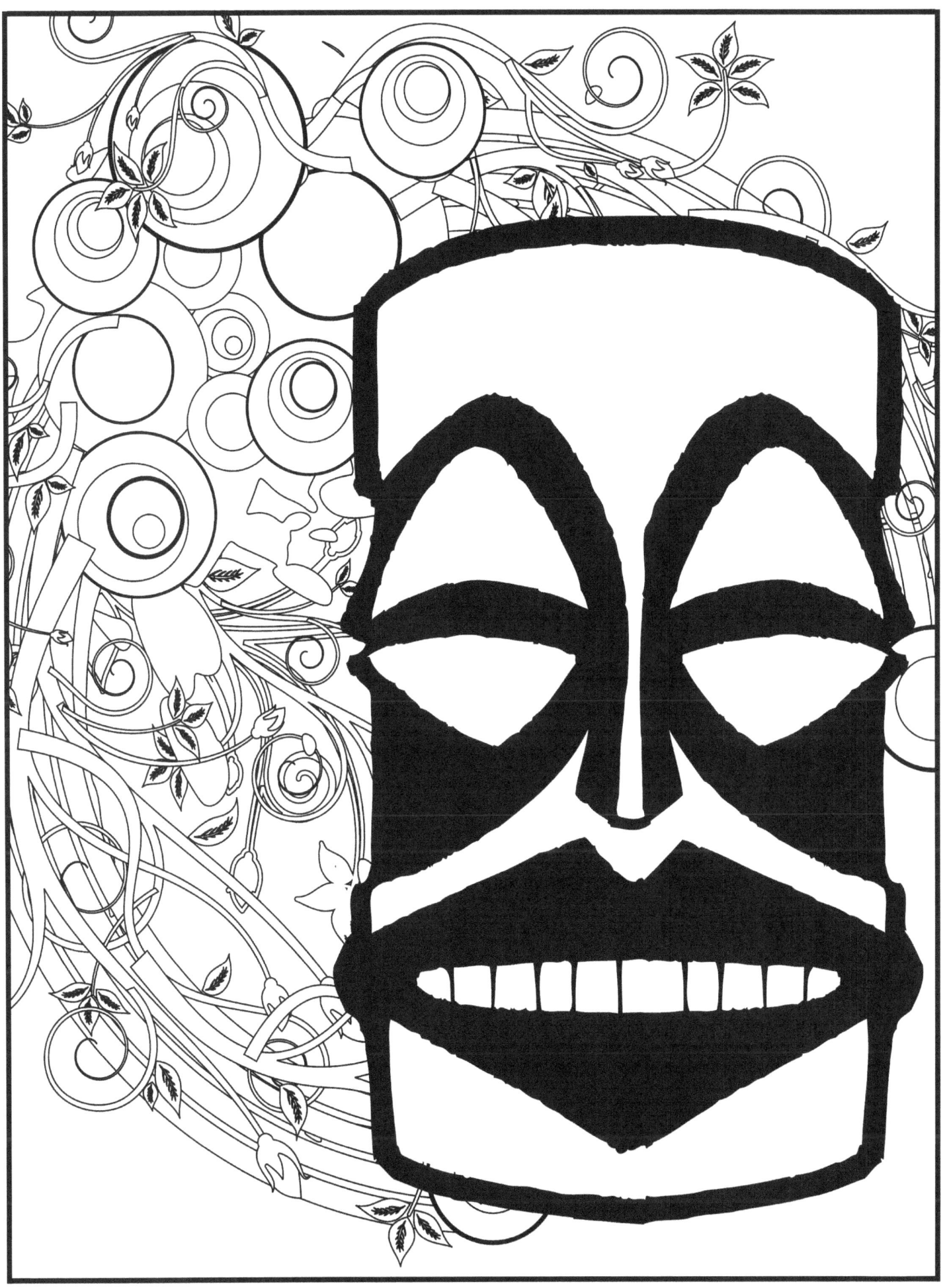

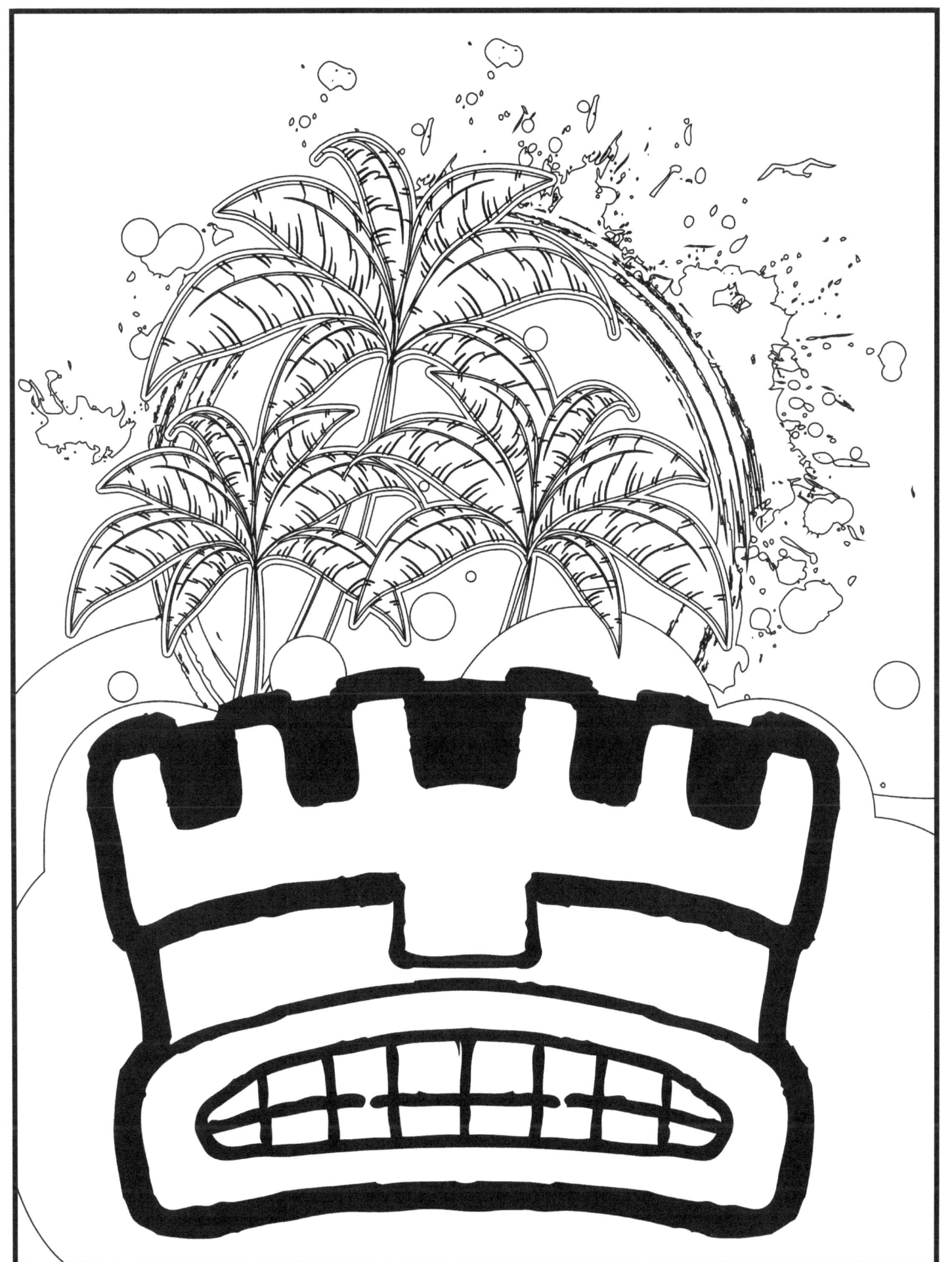

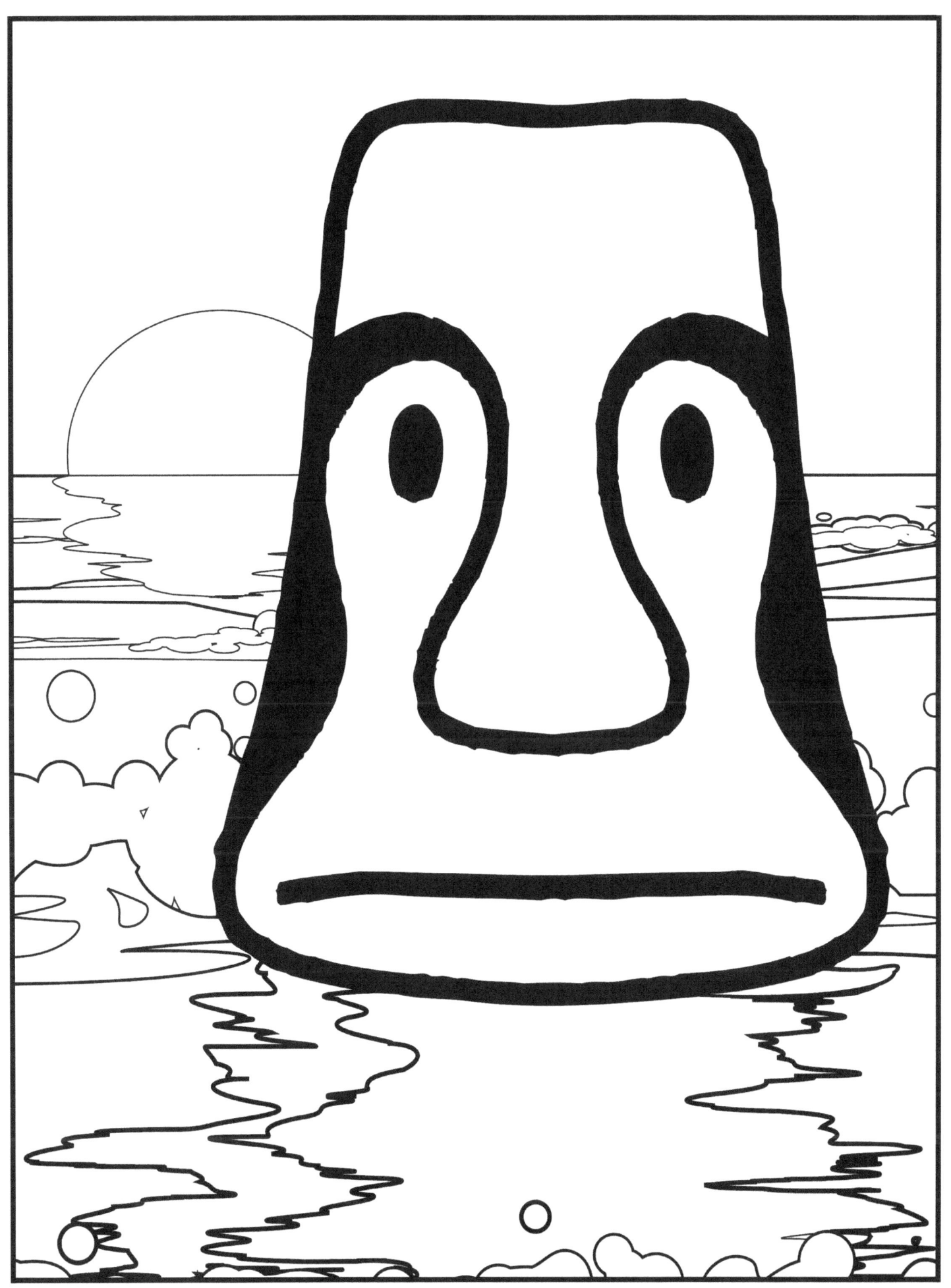

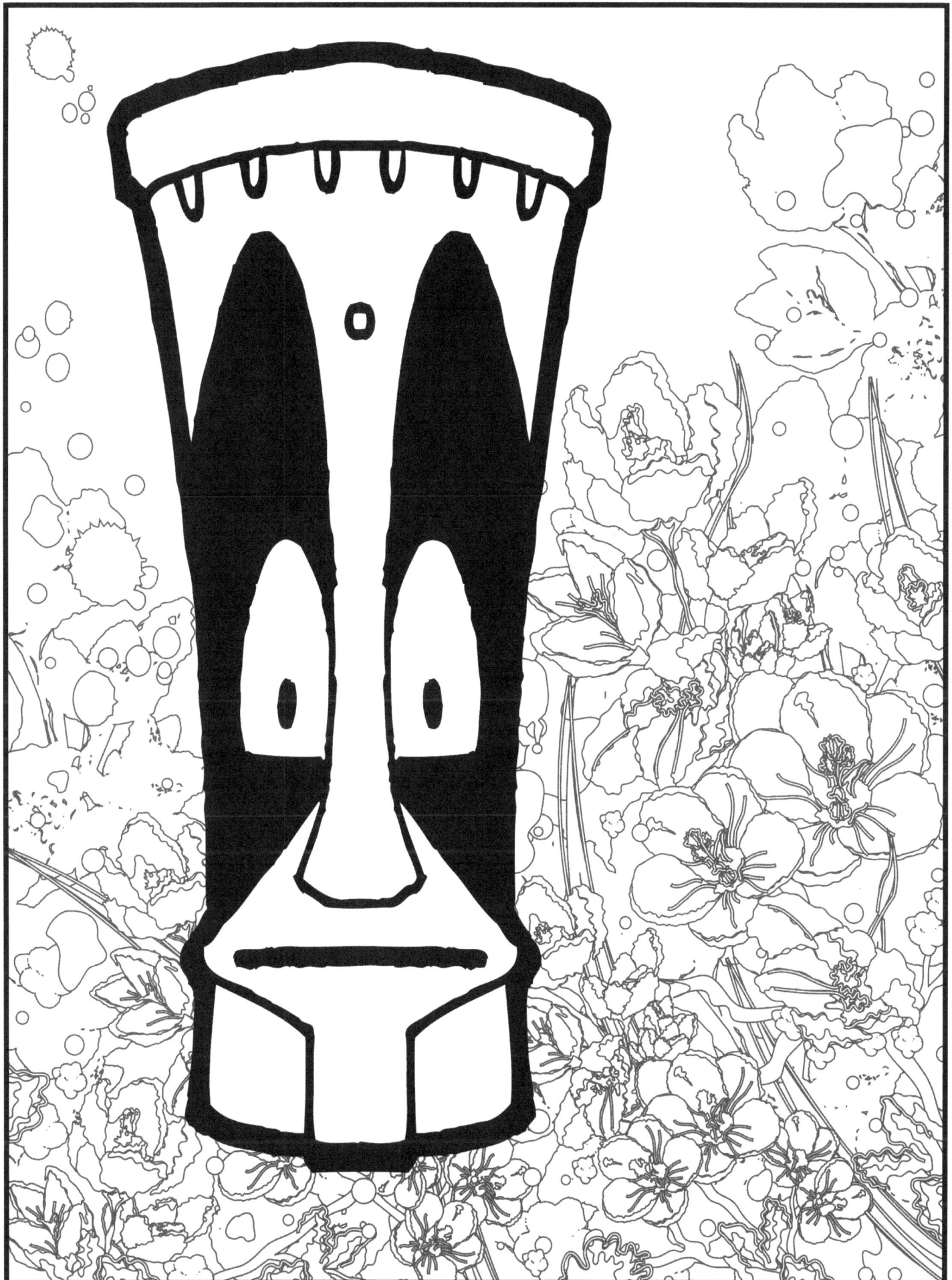

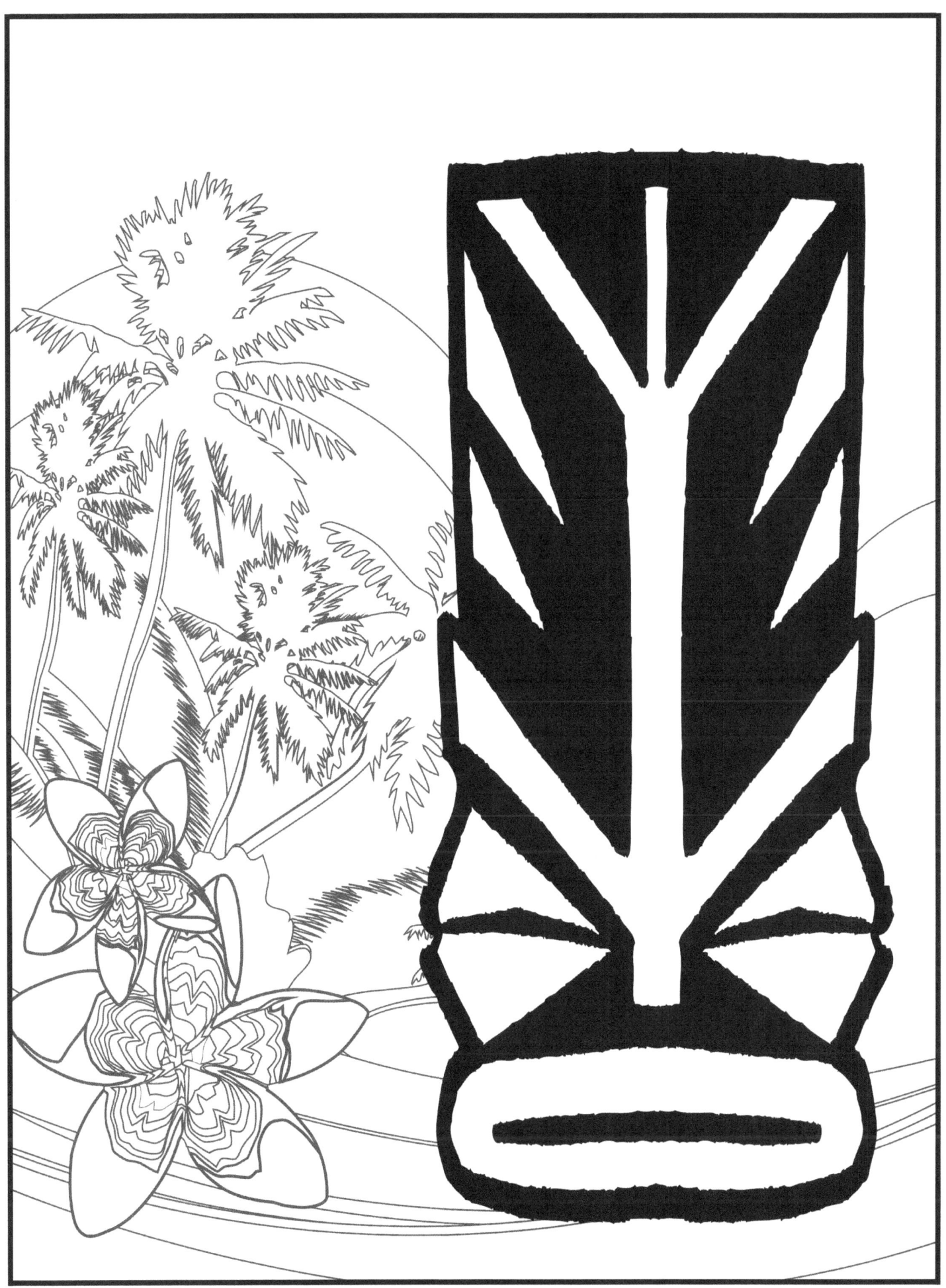

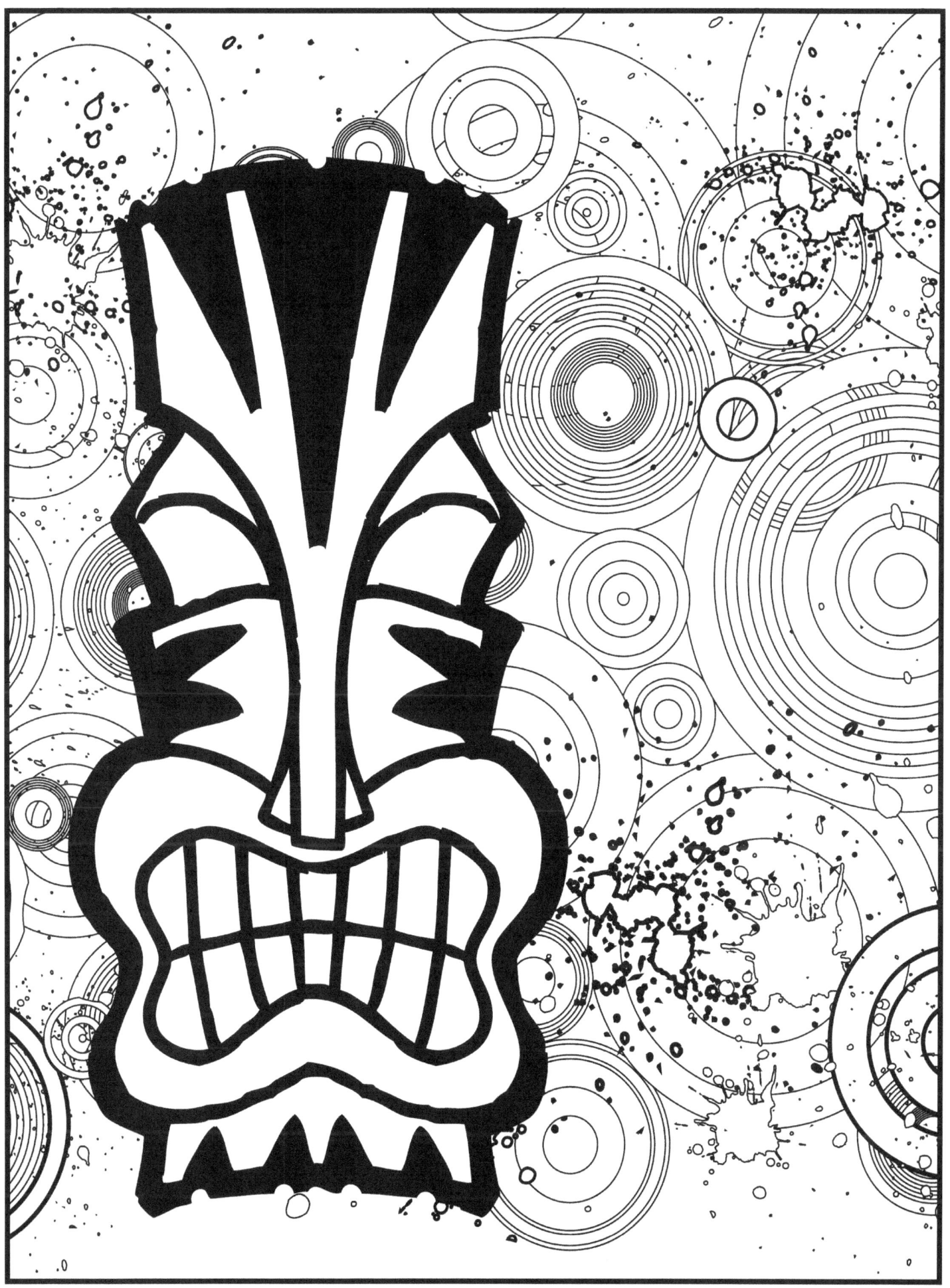

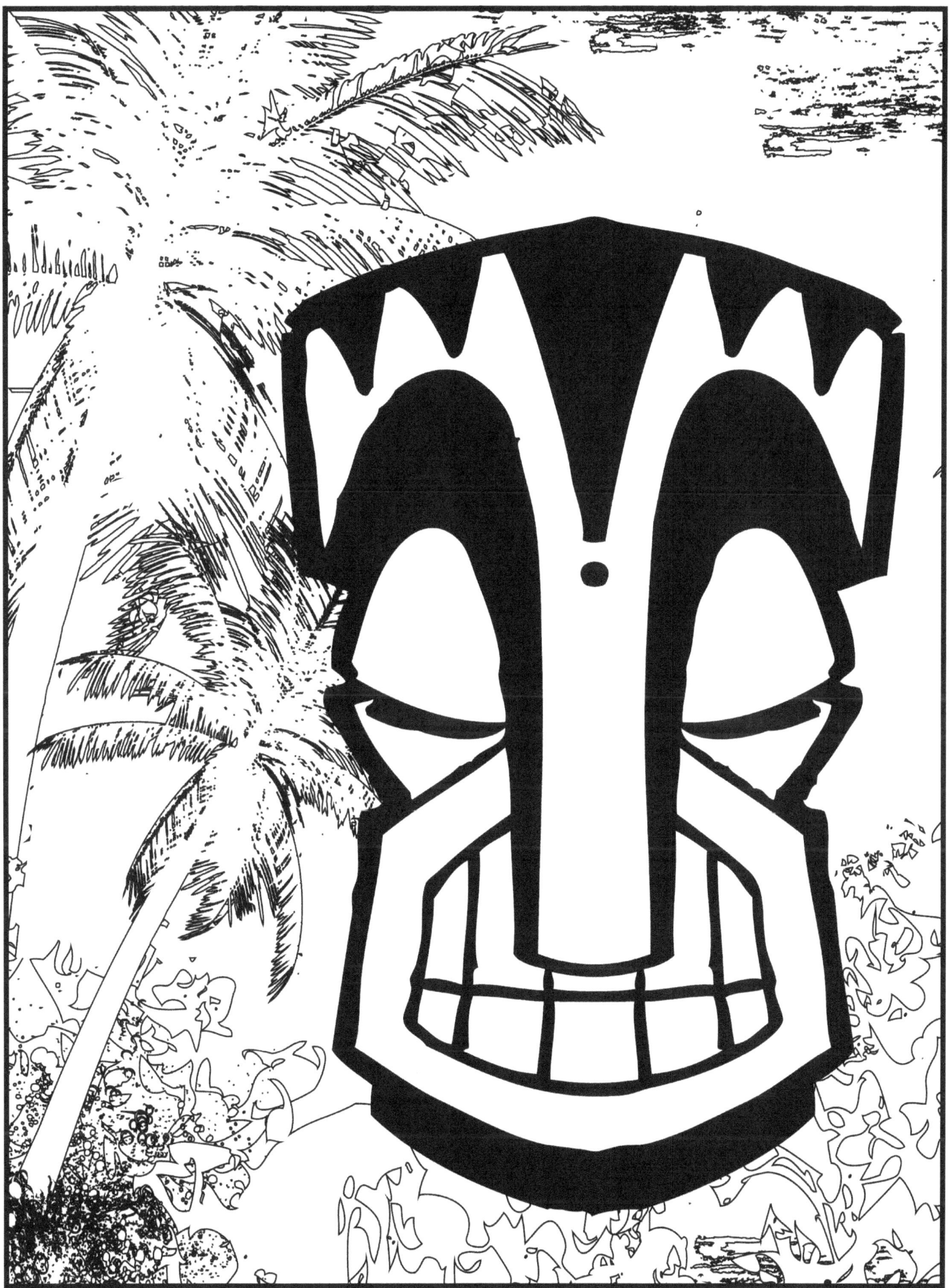

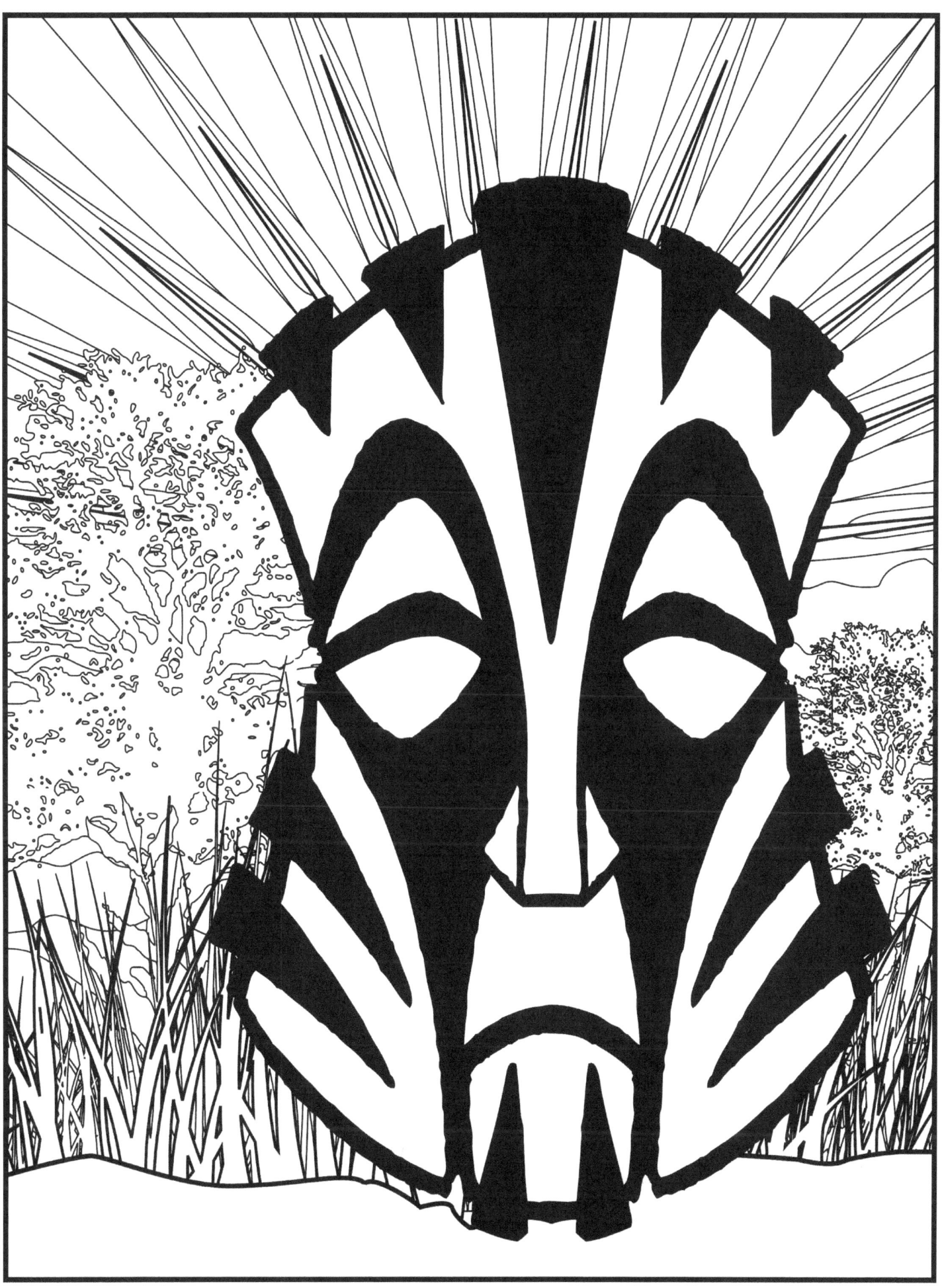

www.ingramcontent.com/pod-product-compliance
Lightning Source LLC
Chambersburg PA
CBHW081235170526
45165CB00009B/3057